house beautiful
KITCHENS

house beautiful
KITCHENS

The Editors of
House Beautiful Magazine

Louis Oliver Gropp, Editor in Chief
Margaret Kennedy, Editor

Text by Carol Sama Sheehan

HEARST BOOKS
NEW YORK

Library of Congress Cataloging-in-Publication Data

House Beautiful.

House beautiful kitchens / the editors of House beautiful
magazine: text by Carol Sama Sheehan.

p.   cm.

ISBN 0-688-10623-4

1. Kitchens. 2. Interior decoration.I. House beautiful. II. Title.
III. Title: Kitchens.

NK2117.K5S54 1993   92-39690

747.7'97--dc20   CIP

Printed in Singapore

First Edition

1   2   3   4   5   6   7   8   9   1 0

Edited by Laurie Orseck
Designed by Michelle Wiener
Produced by Smallwood & Stewart, Inc., New York

CONTENTS

Part I: Kitchen Styles

Part II: Elements of Design

FORM AND FUNCTION
53

STORAGE SOLUTIONS
75

SURFACES AND FINISHES
101

DECORATIVE TOUCHES
123

FOREWORD

During my childhood, family holidays and vacations were usually spent on the Indiana farms where my parents had grown up, and the favorite gathering place in each was always the kitchen. Those rooms were neither particularly well designed nor even workable, but they were always filled with amazing tastes and delicious aromas, and best of all they were presided over by the grandmothers I loved. I'm sure my sister and I were often in the way as they toiled in their far from easy workrooms, but they never indicated they would want us to be anywhere else.

The tradition continues to this day. We all love to congregate in the kitchen; it is where we get the sustenance we need. Fortunately, we now design these rooms with some recognition of the myriad activities and groups of people that assemble there. And now, whether a kitchen presents a contemporary or traditional face, the best include miracle-producing equipment, cabinets with amazing storage, generous and efficient food preparation areas, and enough space for an island or table for informal meals or homework.

My grandmothers would marvel at the kitchens we now photograph for the pages of *House Beautiful*. I can only hope these new rooms nourish their occupants as time spent in my grandmothers' kitchens nourished me.

Louis Oliver Gropp
Editor in Chief

house beautiful
KITCHENS

INTRODUCTION

The colonial "keeping room" was the original heart of the home, where a large open hearth served as its principal heat source. It was there that all cooking was done, and socializing took place around the communal table. Later, as Americans became more prosperous and houses grew in size, the kitchen was moved to a separate room, sometimes even to a separate building.

In the course of time, kitchens were incorporated into residential design, and cooking was finally given a room of its own, albeit at the back of the house as a rule, and with few if any frills or creature comforts. Well-to-do families hardly ever stepped into the kitchen, leaving it to their help to deal with the task. And in more modest households, the room was off limits to visitors, where the family's baking and cooking chores went on from morning to night.

The purely functional role and lowly status of the kitchen meant that this room received little attention from architects and decorators, who concentrated their attention on more visible spaces such as the parlor or formal dining room. With electrification, the kitchen was finally taken seriously as a workplace that required some planning. Often, however, the resulting space resembled a laboratory where efficiency and sanitation came before all other considerations, and sometimes it was hard to find a place just to sit.

Today all that has changed. Not only has the kitchen moved to the center of the house, at least figuratively; its essential character has changed as well. From a peripheral space where one person did the cooking, the kitchen has become a hub where several family members can pitch in with meal preparation and chores, and where many other activities take place, ranging from children's homework to enjoying music or the latest videos for the whole family. In an age when ceremonial dining occasions and formal entertaining have given way to informality, the kitchen has in some ways usurped the social functions of the living room and dining room as well.

The result of all these new pressures on the kitchen is exciting. Demands for a room that provides comfort as well as convenience, style as well as good design, and personality as well as function are being met by manufacturers, kitchen planners, remodelers, and decorators with a host of new materials, new layouts, new ideas. With *House Beautiful Kitchens*, you can take your first steps toward realizing the kitchen of your dreams.

chapter 1

SLEEK CONTEMPORARY

The modern kitchen was born when the icebox gave way to the refrigerator in the first part of this century, and by the 1950s had become a sleek, if antiseptic, space. Today's kitchen is better equipped than ever, but it does not have to sacrifice atmosphere or style for efficiency. While its technology delivers first-class service to the myriad needs of contemporary families, it can still be as personal and inviting as every other room in the house.

With economy of design, the contemporary kitchen converts normally "dead" space into innovative, usable work and storage areas. Materials like thin but durable laminates and the development of Eurostyle flush-mounted cabinets with concealed hinges and touch-latch closures have played a major role in giving kitchens a seamless, "fitted" look. White is the color of choice, but to avoid what could be construed as a lack of warmth, natural light is maximized via skylights and reflective surfaces like ceramic tile, stainless steel, and glass.

Even with its high degree of organization and coordinated appearance, contemporary kitchen design leaves plenty of room for homeowners to personalize the scheme. By using different surfaces such as tile, vinyl, plastic laminates, wood, marble, and granite in the same palette, and introducing bold touches of color ~ in a backsplash design, a cheerful pottery collection, or even a few potted plants ~ sleek contemporary can be as warm and inviting as it is cool and efficient.

Sophisticated renovation
for a family kitchen

Childhood memories helped transform a dark and antiquated kitchen, last remodeled 25 years earlier, into a sleek, shining example of a room where an entire family can relax, prepare meals, eat, and even work out.

The pre-World War II apartment building in New York City that a young family calls home came equipped with such desirable architectural features as 10-foot ceilings, hardwood floors, plaster moldings, and a handsome working fireplace. The kitchen, however, was about as interesting as a brown suit ~ spacious but dark, dominated by a bank of wood cabinets with a cooking peninsula that jutted awkwardly into the room.

The wife came to understand the kitchen from a cook's point of view after living with its limitations for some time. Work surfaces were scattered, requiring too much back-and-forth movement for even the simplest tasks. The cooktop was poorly located, cabinets protruded unevenly into the room, and lighting was inadequate. "I wanted the kitchen to be bright and cheery," says the owner, who turned to her sister-in-law, architect Kathryn McGraw Berry, to redesign the space. The plan Berry developed offered a scope of improvements for the family: more usable counter space, room and equipment for two people to cook at the same time, a center work island complete with a marble top for pastry-making, and more accessible storage. Along with these improvements, the homeowners envisioned a bright and inviting space that would serve as the center of family life.

"We were very fortunate," the architect observes, "in that we started out with a pretty large space and could make it even bigger ~ 300 square feet ~ by incorporating space from

The cooktop's stainless steel surface meets restaurant standards for durability, heat tolerance, and ease of cleaning (opposite). A custom-made vent hood of the same material adds an architectural focal point as well as serving an important function.

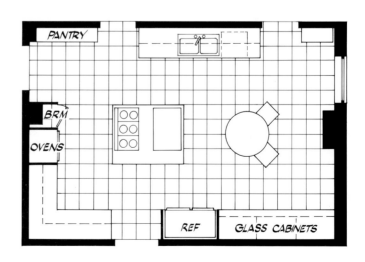

a former maid's quarters." All that now remains of the remodeled 1960s kitchen is the refrigerator.

One of the kitchen's most glaring defects was a failure to exploit the sole window in the room. Nothing could improve its indifferent view, but its potential for bringing in light was untapped.

"In an urban setting, light is all important," Berry explains. Before the renovation, there was no place for the light to go, except to disappear into the dark surfaces of the cave-like room. Now all surfaces reflect light: painted white walls and cabinets, laminate and glass-fronted doors, glass shelves, white laminate countertops, vinyl flooring, white ceramic tile backsplash, a work island topped with stainless steel, and a custom venting hood of the same material. The result is dramatic: "Light bounces off everything now," says the architect.

Pushing back the sink wall two feet resulted in space in which cabinets and appliances could all be aligned. Sleek and contemporary flush-mounted cabinets create a clean and efficient look. In order to avoid a monotonous industrial effect, architect Berry mixed open shelving with glass and solid cabinet fronts. "I like playing around with a combination of solid spaces and voids. I'm very much of the clean-kitchen school," she says. "I don't like to see things left all over."

The enlarged space also resulted in an improved traffic pattern, as well as ample

Reflective surfaces ~
glass, stainless steel,
and ceramic tile ~ make
the most of the room's
natural light (opposite).

Impressionistic blues
and yellows, inspired
by the owner's collection
of Monet china, give the
kitchen its uplifting color

scheme (above). Cushiony
vinyl floor tile repeats the
colors of the ceramic tile.

21

space for a tailor-made work island. Its ingenious design incorporates open shelves for cookbooks and daily tableware, cabinets with solid doors to keep less-used dishware and equipment out of sight, and wire shelving to hold a collection of copper pots and serving pieces.

The coordinated use of blue and yellow in the tile backsplash and the vinyl tile floor gives the kitchen its special sparkle.

"I tried to evoke a feeling of a visit to Grandmother's kitchen," says the architect, "but for a very modern family."

The wife reports contentedly, "My husband likes to ride his exercise bike in here, our daughter keeps her toy stove in the corner, and our son uses the area around the work island as his race track. It's the perfect family kitchen."

In a kitchen designed to serve as well as prepare food, no space goes unused. Open shelves under the work island are reserved for the cook's workhorse pots and pans, and in an out-of-reach corner a doorless cabinet showcases the homowners' favorite possessions.

Open-plan
model of efficiency

t he large, family-friendly, contemporary kitchen shown on these pages is the unique vision of designer Ristomatti Ratia, whose creations for Marimekko, the studio his mother founded, are known around the world.

Ratia's goal in designing this kitchen was to put a host of modern conveniences in a setting with the soul of a Scandinavian farmhouse ~ "one that brings people together instead of isolating them," he explains. Not surprisingly, Ratia's family home in his native Finland boasts a kitchen with the same multifaceted purpose and personality.

Besides the basics, this open-plan kitchen incorporates a working fireplace, a computer station, and an entertainment center; a greenhouse floods the room with natural light and provides flowers and herbs for year-round color and flavor, in much the same way the kitchen garden serves a farm family. In this room, a multitude of activities is possible without sacrificing a pleasing sense of order. The designer explains, "The room can handle everything ~ children at computer games, shopping bags, dinner party preparations ~ without ever looking really messy because the heavy structure of the beams takes your eye up and over whatever may be on the counter or table."

The operational end of the room looks clean and uncluttered because of a number of

A tile-topped dining table and laminate surfaces for countertops and cabinets are practical choices that impart a contemporary look to a hard-working kitchen (opposite). A shelf suspended over the work island keeps everyday dishware handy. A spice rack on rollers, attached to the underside of overhead cabinets, moves where the cook needs it.

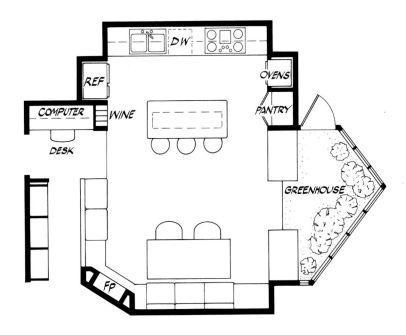

25

An alcove in the open-plan kitchen encourages family members to bring their homework and favorite music into the cook's room (left).

With wheels on one end, the dining table can be easily moved (opposite). Rolled in front of the fire, it seats six or more in an intimate dinner setting. The tiled platform, with the addition of loose cushions and futon, becomes either a banquette or spare bed.

carefully planned details. Recessed appliances, a built-in pantry concealed behind doors, and frameless custom cabinets create an unbroken line in the layout. Room for a wine rack with a four-case capacity was created in an otherwise useless partial wall.

A neutral color scheme of warm beiges and whites also contributes to the contemporary feeling of the room. A subtle mix of textures makes the kitchen as visually interesting as it is practical. Smooth laminate surfaces were chosen for cabinets, refrigerator door panels, and countertops in the work area. A crisp ceramic tile covers the tabletop, seating platform, and kitchen floor. The oak flooring in the living room and dining area was given a pickled finish, a soft effect achieved by brushing on white paint, then wiping it to allow the natural grain of the wood to show through. Glare is not a problem in spite of the many white surfaces: The daylight that pours through skylights and greenhouse walls suffuses the generous dimensions of the 22-by-28-foot room with a soft glow.

As in most effective kitchen plans, the cooking area is protected from traffic, but strategic placement of the work island still allows the cook to enjoy the company of family and friends or keep a watchful eye on young children. "The room was designed to promote joyful family gatherings," says Ratia, "children settling down to homework while parents cook informal fireside dinners with guests, teenage sleepovers with futons spread out on the tiled platform ledge. The possibilities are endless."

A raftered ceiling, skylights, and the glass walls of the greenhouse make a large room seem even more spacious and airy. Pickled oak flooring and a wide variety of neutral-colored surfaces help to unify a space that has distinct divisions. Painted oak bankers' chairs lend an old-fashioned touch, while very modern tubular-steel stools turn the work island into a breakfast nook or snack counter.

chapter 2

TIMELESS COUNTRY

Perhaps because of nostalgia for the communal and supportive nature of the colonial hearth, the country kitchen has always enjoyed enormous popularity, and never more so than today. The key element in any interpretation of the country kitchen is comfort, a prerequisite in a room when people are as important as pots and pans. This homey area is often filled to the brim with hardworking treasures. Glass-fronted cabinets, plate racks, and reproduction kitchen furniture help to create an "unstructured" atmosphere with ample room for piles of boots, wet dogs, and other aspects of daily family life, whether down on the farm or at home in the suburbs.

In its latest incarnation, the country kitchen often sports a foreign accent, as ideas and materials from abroad help homeowners invest the room with English, Scandinavian, European, or Latin flavor and character. But there's nothing gilded or glossy about any of these versions. Cabinets are stripped plain and hand-rubbed or hand-painted. Floors are made of solid materials like brick, stone, quarry tile, slate, or hand-stenciled wood. A beamed ceiling, elegant Palladian windows, or a prize wood-burning range may provide the finishing touch.

The beauty of a country kitchen is in its versatility and flexibility. Flea-market finds and primitive antiques can coexist happily. The room may evoke the spare beauty of Shaker design or the friendly clutter of Grandma's attic, but it always says "Welcome."

Old-world charm
in a modern setting

Craftsman-built cupboards, boldly painted green and embellished with decorative arches, function as furniture (opposite). The one above houses a collection of colorful Portuguese plates. Mullioned glass doors, pulls intentionally left natural to show wear over time, and marble countertops and backsplash lend a period look to the room. Stencils on the cupboard peaks add a friendly note.

C raftsmanship, color, and clever design turned a newly built kitchen into a room that looks as if it came out of a country farmhouse from another era. "The client asked for a house that looked as if it had been built years earlier," explains designer Carl D'Aquino, so everything brought into the house was chosen to guide the eye past the newness of construction.

For the kitchen, old and new materials were skillfully blended. Salvaged wooden beams, left in their original state, were installed in the ceiling, and unmatched chairs were used for the seating. Cabinets were made to resemble cupboards, and a wooden worktable supported on legs carved to resemble urns was added. "The table was designed to look like an old piece you might come across at auction. For all its wackiness, it's really very practical," notes the designer, who also equipped it with handy drawers for storing cooking utensils and a thick fossil-stone top to handle the cook's prep work.

The kitchen cabinets emit old-world charm with their glass-paned fronts, carved shelf brackets, marble countertops, and fanciful peaks that soar into the recesses of the vaulted ceiling. With all the appliances built into the furniture-like facade on two walls, the impression is of a room dominated by wood even though most of the appliances are faced with stainless steel. The cabinetry helps create a cottage-like atmosphere and taps out-of-the-way places, like the space above the refrigerator, to serve as congenial showcases for pitchers, teapots, and bowls.

Painted surfaces have always played a key role in endowing a kitchen with country charm, and this room is no exception. Originally, milk paints provided instant decorating in colonial keeping rooms and were used on walls, floors, and furniture to hide defects in the wood or mismatched planks. Here, paint was used artfully to take the decor back in time. It also unifies the kitchen and dining room, which are separated by a pantry. Almost every piece of furniture and surface was painted ~ in fact, seven coats of paint were applied to the dining room hutch to achieve its exalted antique look. Kitchen cabinets and wainscoting were painted seafoam green, and their interiors were drenched with an intense blue just short of cobalt. Even the kitchen floor got a shot of color. "We found cement tile in Mexico that can be colored by mixing pigment into the materials," says D'Aquino. "The effect is the look of a tile you might find in an old Provençal kitchen ~ handmade instead of manufactured."

To humanize the new space even further, model sailboats once used on a pond in Central Park are now anchored on walls and tabletops, a humorous and engaging note of special interest for the youngster in the family. "It was a way of adding 'art' to the house without making a big investment," says the designer.

By paying attention to the details of living as well as to the details of space, D'Aquino and his colleagues Geordie Humphreys, Nina Rowan, and architect Paul Laird imposed country character on a spanking new kitchen.

The new pine hutch in the dining room was given seven coats of paint, each a different color, to achieve its antique look. The old bench sports original paint while the painted spindle-back chairs are reproductions. A toy boat navigates through this house near the ocean.

Something borrowed, something new

A corner of the kitchen is transformed into a family gathering area with the addition of a built-in banquette, maple-topped café table, and cane chairs (left). The newly added bay window fills the room with abundant natural light and garden views. A stainless-steel vent hood was custom-made to look as though it came out of a turn-of-the-century kitchen (above).

i t is tempting, when remodeling an old kitchen sadly in need of an update, simply to gut the interior and start from scratch. Sometimes, however, a more moderate approach makes more sense, especially if a room has vintage architectural elements worth preserving.

Such was the case in this 1885 California farmhouse kitchen. The owners collaborated with architect Michael Rex to develop a plan that would replace the worn-out range and homely cast-iron sink but preserve the simple charm of the old room. "We couldn't salvage any of the original working parts of the kitchen in the renovation, but we still managed to remain true to the house's heritage," says the architect.

Often successful remodeling projects are planned and executed in stages. This one, in fact, called for three distinct phases, which affected virtually the entire house. Phase one was primarily cosmetic in nature, designed to make the house livable. In the second phase, the basement was converted into a living space, including a home office and bath. Phase three called for relocating the existing dining room and kitchen areas into one large country room measuring approximately 200 square feet. The last stage also included a two-story addition on the rear of the house, with an upstairs family room off the new kitchen.

To convert the kitchen into an efficient area for the owners and their two small daughters, Rex applied what he called his

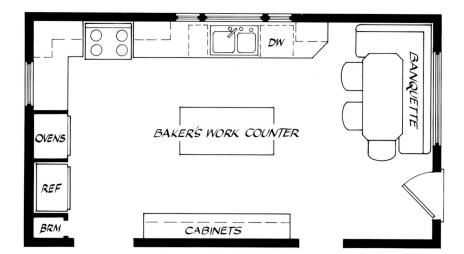

OVENS

REF

BRM

BAKER'S WORK COUNTER

DW

BANQUETTE

CABINETS

"Farmer John" rule. "I wanted to keep the design honest and not take away from the simplicity of the farmhouse style," he explains, "so I came up with the idea of measuring everything we wanted to do against the ability and simple taste of a typical self-sufficient farmer to do it."

For example, the tall windows that give the room so much scale and drama were built with wooden frames and finished with a grid of small panes, resulting in a window a farmer might have installed by hand. "We added a flattened arch to the window over the sink," the architect notes. "It's not as sophisticated as the Palladian window form it suggests ~ it's more like an arched window a farmer would have crafted."

A local carpenter built the kitchen cabinets to look like furniture rather than like boxes hung on a wall. To achieve this effect, the wall above the cabinets was furred down and a cornice added along the top of the walls. Then, instead of spray-painting the woodwork, surfaces were given several coats of enamel paint, brushed on by hand.

Determined to create a comfortable, country alcove within the room, the architect designed a cushioned banquette under the existing picture window. "It's where the kids not only eat dinner, but have their after-school snacks and do their homework," he notes. Another important feature was supplied by the wife of the household when she came home with an old Parisian baker's counter she'd found in an antiques shop. It was in horrible condition but had lots of handmade character and proved to be a wonderful work island. It was something of a splurge and a gamble, but it was the kind of finishing touch that makes the big difference in any room.

With fresh colors, abundant light, and "Farmer John" details throughout, it's no surprise that this country kitchen is so welcoming. "When people walk into this room," says the architect, "they just smile."

The centerpiece of the
room is a pine counter,
incised with a symbolic
sheaf of wheat. Formerly
a fixture in an old
French boulangerie, it
serves as a work island
for all kinds of tasks,
from baking pies to
arranging flowers. Pine
shelving in the cabinets
subtly tie together
the wood floor and wood
counter. An adjoining
laundry room was
connected to the main
kitchen area to make room
for the conveniences
and comforts required by
a young family of four.

chapter 3

TAILOR-MADE

The kitchen specially tailored to the unique needs and tastes of the cook, homeowner, or entire family can take as many different forms as there are people. In today's world of two-income families and single parents, many kitchens have become all-purpose rooms where cooking, eating, entertaining, and just "hanging out" are all welcome activities. Such kitchens actually appropriate roles traditionally assigned to other areas in the house, most notably the den or family room and the formal dining room.

In decor the specialty kitchen may be ultramodern or pleasantly old-fashioned; in function it can satisfy almost any personality or requirement, from the professional chef to the two-cook household, from the media-oriented family to the homeowner in need of extra office space.

For the gourmet cook used to exacting standards, desirable features might include a commercial range, an extra-deep sink for handling big stockpots, and stainless-steel work surfaces. The ideal kitchen for a large family might include technologically advanced appliances for meal preparation and cleanup, desk and computer for a home office and homework center, and video and stereo equipment for adults and children alike. In a house without a dining room, a tailor-made kitchen might just mean enough space and comfortable seating for dinner parties for family and friends.

A place for everything ~
even the kitchen sink

a kitchen that harnesses virtually all the innovations modern technology has to offer serves not only as a place to eat, but as an office and entertainment center as well. Such a room was designed by Barbara Ross and Barbara Schwartz to address the complicated needs of many of today's families. "We put everything into the design ~ stereo system, videocassette recorder, oversize furniture, technologically advanced appliances, computer, and even a Japanese storage chest ~ to satisfy the lifestyle of a busy young household of four," the designers explain.

Today's typical family expects a kitchen to work on many levels ~ a place to congregate and work as well as to cook. Houses built in previous decades featured separate dens, living rooms, and formal dining rooms. In today's home, the kitchen has absorbed the role and function of these rooms by means of its flexible floor plan.

Fitting everything into one "great room" requires a special eye for turning a cavernous space into comfortable quarters. Adding a distinctive architectural feature is one way to achieve continuity with the other rooms in the house. "We had arches designed for each entrance to the room to echo those in other parts of the house and give the space an architectural grace that makes it more than a

A "three-in-one kitchen" comes complete with a computer workstation, where the checkbook can be balanced or homework done when the cook is not using it to retrieve recipes. With cabinetry made to look like furniture and framed art on the walls, the room is designed to meet a family's social and recreational needs as well as serve its traditional function.

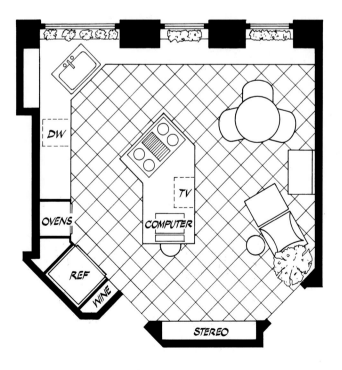

Natural materials and a stylish checkerboard floor help to make the room warm and inviting (left). Appliance doors were paneled in ash to match custom cabinets, while built-in ovens were specified in black glass to coordinate with the black granite countertops.

Entertainment options include a built-in stereo system, built-in television, and VCR, with comfortable upholstered front-row seating.

Convenience and ease reign as open shelves keep cookbooks and casserole dishes handy over the corner sink, which is only steps away from the cooktop island. Spacious counters on either side of the sink make it possible for several people to help with meal preparation without bumping into each other. Under-cabinet task lighting and a large overhead fixture chase shadows from the countertop and work island.

kitchen," notes Schwartz. A certain softness was also desirable in a room full of hard surfaces. The edges of the cabinets and countertops were rounded and cream-colored tiles were specified for backsplashes. Instead of painting the walls, the decorators covered them in a linen fabric that warms up the room and absorbs sounds as well. An upholstered chaise longue and the checkerboard floor pattern are elegant notes in a kitchen hospitable to all kinds of activities, whether balancing the checkbook, catching up on homework, or watching Julia Child prepare a soufflé on videotape.

As the room evolved, the natural materials the designers selected ~ white ash cabinetry, black granite countertops, black-and-white ceramic floor tiles ~ took on a Japanese aesthetic. "That's why we chose accents like the oriental chest and the dining chairs, which are technically Scandinavian in design but show a strong Japanese influence," Ross explains. Translucent window shades and the hanging light fixture with its rice paper shades continue the oriental motif. The black-and-white still lifes selected for the walls also help to soften the hardworking character of an extremely well equipped kitchen.

Planning a work area in which more than one person can pitch in to prepare a meal is another priority for most working couples. Here it is met with long, spacious counters on either side of the corner sink. The center island and its cooktop provide the primary workstation, one that is compact and efficient. The computer built into the island can be swiveled to face the cooktop, allowing the chef of the day to call up a favorite recipe or menu on the screen.

Specialty of the house

An extra-long counter, with pull-out storage drawers and a niche for holding colorful serving vessels, supplies ample room for prep work or pastry-making (above).

Glass cabinet doors, wall hooks, and an open shelf under the work island help chef Alice Waters keep her home kitchen (opposite) as well organized as her restaurant. The two butcher-block workstations double as snack counters when stools are pulled up.

"t he most important room in a house, to me, is the kitchen," says celebrated chef Alice Waters, whose simple, imaginative cooking has made Chez Panisse, her Berkeley, California, restaurant, a culinary landmark. When the time came to renovate her own kitchen, Waters acted on this belief. The result is a congenial and practical space that harks back to another time in its decor and reliance on hand tools and skills rather than gadgets and contraptions. Now the biggest room in the 1907 Victorian bungalow, the kitchen used to be, at 15 by 15 feet, one of the smallest and least efficient. Waters consulted with an architect friend to design a kitchen that would retain the room's old-fashioned high ceilings and tall windows and still address the needs and desires of a professional cook: built-in brick ovens, outsize sink, generous work surfaces, and see-at-a-glance storage.

By building out onto the back of the property, the best parts of the old kitchen were saved and the existing space was more than doubled. Also central to the redesign was a fireplace. Wood-burning brick ovens were built into the chimney, perfect for baking pizza and bread and for grilling foods on a spit. A copper sink, measuring 40 inches long, 20 inches wide, and 10 inches deep, is big enough to hide dirty dishes.

Waters determinedly sought out materials that would show wear, but not tear, over time.

"I really like a kitchen to show its age, to have work surfaces with patina," she says. For her countertops, she found an African slate that "doesn't ever look dirty and is porous enough to soak up water." The original oak cupboards sport new glass-paned doors.

Waters is a firm believer in unadulterated natural food, and now she has an unadulterated kitchen in which to prepare and enjoy the fruits of her talent.

A vintage Oriole enamel cookstove is equipped with two ovens, a plate warmer, and a nook for holding bread while it rises (above).

A slate-top table, a mixed group of comfortable old chairs by the hearth, and generous views of the backyard garden make this kitchen the most popular room in the house (right).

chapter 4

FORM AND FUNCTION

How many steps do you take to make a cup of tea in your own kitchen? The answer depends on the efficiency of your kitchen layout and the usefulness, in terms of your daily needs, of all its component parts.

Whether building a new kitchen from scratch or renovating an existing room with its own set of assets and drawbacks, the goal is to end up with a workplace that allows for meal planning, preparation, and serving with a minimum of fuss ~ the place for aerobic workouts is the gym or dance studio, not the kitchen. At the same time, that workplace should be a pleasure to be in on its own terms, one designed with flair and personality and bearing an appropriate and organic relationship to neighboring spaces in the house.

The layout of the kitchen, and the resulting patterns, are the designer's first consideration. Small kitchens should take advantage of compact appliances such as apartment-size dishwashers and cooktops; the installation of microwave ovens at eye level frees up valuable countertop work space for food preparation. Full-size refrigerators are designed to fit flush with cabinets. Large kitchens must also be designed to work smoothly, in many cases by allocating zones to specific tasks, including menu planning, food preparation, serving, and clean-up. Both task and ambient lighting can virtually transform the look and efficiency of a kitchen.

Grand central station
in an urban loft

Converting what used to be a hard-nosed industrial space into a comfortable home is more of a challenge than most people realize. Too often the volume of space overwhelms the floor plan, and essential rooms like the kitchen are consigned to one small corner.

Sometimes, however, the remodeling goes just right. When architect Michael Rubin was commissioned to tackle a 2,500-square-foot

loft in a former Manhattan printing plant, he managed to preserve the offbeat glamour of the industrial space while giving a young family of four all the comforts of home.

In the overall renovation scheme, the architect kept the shell of the original loft space intact ~ columns, ceiling, and exterior walls. He had the exterior walls and columns painted white and the new walls green to heighten the contrast between the domestic apartment and its industrial framework. To "tame" the interior space, he selected pale wood and glass for the furniture, then used Japanese-style screens to serve as dividers between the rooms.

The kitchen was, literally, central to Rubin's success. "Once we made the decision to place it in the middle of the space, everything else fell into place," he explains. He positioned the room as a highly accessible 160-square-foot work island in the cen-

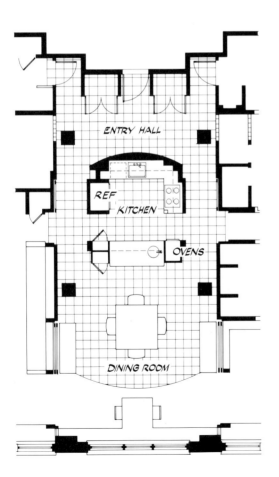

ENTRY HALL

REF

KITCHEN

OVENS

DINING ROOM

Situating the kitchen and adjoining dining area in the middle of the loft was key to making the space efficient and livable. The "room" was designed so that it would not detract from the loft feeling. Downlights mounted as sconces are controlled by dimmers to provide bright light for cooking and low light for dining.

ter of the loft. A square structure made of birch with an arching roof under the taller loft ceiling, it has its own distinct identity. "In a way, it's like a great room divider. When you enter the loft, you have to walk around the curved back of the wall. Then you become aware of the kitchen as a room that 'floats' in the middle." A large, generously windowed area adjoining the kitchen is both a dining area and a passageway to the living room on one side and master suite on the other. The family often gathers around the big dining table, which basks in the sunlight from south-facing windows.

The pass-through counter between the kitchen and the dining area functions as a buffet bar for entertaining. The counter enables the hosts to have complete access to the working side of the kitchen without ensnaring guests in traffic.

Custom-made cabinets, designed by the architect, are made of birch veneer plywood and provide more than adequate storage. Appliances were chosen as much for their performance as for their sleek appearance. The stylish German range has a vent system that disappears under a wall cabinet when not in use. Instead of a standard 30-inch-deep refrigerator, a 24-inch model was chosen because it can be built in flush with the cabinets. Wall-mounted ovens were selected for the same reason.

Pink Tennessee marble, pretty and practical, covers the floor. As with most of the materials used throughout the loft, it was chosen to suggest the elegance found in staterooms of fin-de-siècle ocean liners. Yet the result is highly contemporary in feeling, without appearing trendy.

The pass-through counter, with a second sink and customized storage for tableware and linens below, is the visual divider between kitchen and dining area (top).

A full complement of wall-hung and base cabinets, plus a tier of drawers, provides ample storage space (above).

In a formerly commercial neighborhood, the kitchen enjoys a fabulous view of the World Trade Center (left). A change in ceiling height tames the expanse of space and creates a small, intimate area for breakfasting. Blond wood louvers allow a glimpse of the impressive loft ceiling above. The dining table, on casters, offers roll-away convenience with impeccable style (below).

Hardworking elegance

an artist as much as a builder, Fu-Tung Cheng of Berkeley, California, took on the challenge of renovating a 20-year-old kitchen whose linoleum floor was its only outstanding feature.

"I was asked to create a kitchen that would be open in feeling, very useful, with plenty of storage, and, last but not least, that would have style," notes Cheng. Ripping out the existing kitchen and starting from scratch, he created a room stamped with originality, texture, and spaciousness. Redesigning the floor plan allowed him the luxury of grouping appliances where they would be the least obtrusive, along one wall and housed in custom-designed cabinetry.

To enhance the feeling of openness in the room, which encompasses about 260 square feet, Cheng replaced the old overhead cabinets with windows and built custom under-counter storage out of vertical-grain fir used both in matching fashion and in counterpoint.

One of the main goals of the renovation was to create a centerpiece for the somewhat awkward space. "There's a big jog in the room created by the garage on one side," Cheng points out. He added a work island in the center of the room, then installed a professional range on the problem wall, in a counter slightly higher than the others in the room. "The change of levels creates another point of interest," he adds. He also designed

Replacing wall-hung cabinets with windows and using only base cabinets for storage gave the kitchen natural light and openness (opposite). A cookbook nook over a broad bank of windows shows what can be done with normally wasted space. Refrigerator, oven, and microwave were installed on one wall, flush with cabinets.

To add interest to a low ceiling, a cove was created and an energy-efficient fluorescent light fixture installed to highlight the recess (left). Elsewhere, low-voltage lamps are used for task lighting and to accentuate the polished surfaces. Outdoor halogen lighting in the vent hood illuminates the commercial range's cooktop with 600-watt brilliance.

the countertops to be deeper than standard ~ 30 inches instead of 25 ~ to keep the scale of the room in balance.

The kitchen also boasts not one but three sinks. Both the largest, for cleaning big pots and pans, and the medium-size one, for rinsing and stacking dishes, are positioned near the dishwasher. A third, small sink, close to the stove, is used for prep work.

The custom design of the cabinets, though expensive, allows beautiful solutions for tricky problems. One of two diagonal corner cabinets located on the stove wall is outfitted with gliders for a pull-out trash basket; the other corner cabinet provides extra storage space. A flour drawer under the peninsula baking center and a pots-and-pans bin under the stove also pull out for handy use. A row of cabinets under a wall of windows serves as a pantry for storing staples. Next to the refrigerator is a pantry closet.

Natural materials always figure prominently in Cheng's kitchen designs, and this one is no exception: The countertops are made of poured concrete.

In the baking peninsula, concrete was poured so that granite could be set into the countertop to accommodate the owner's penchant for pastry-making. The range vent hood benefits from the hand of a builder-artist who turned this utilitarian feature into an object of visual interest.

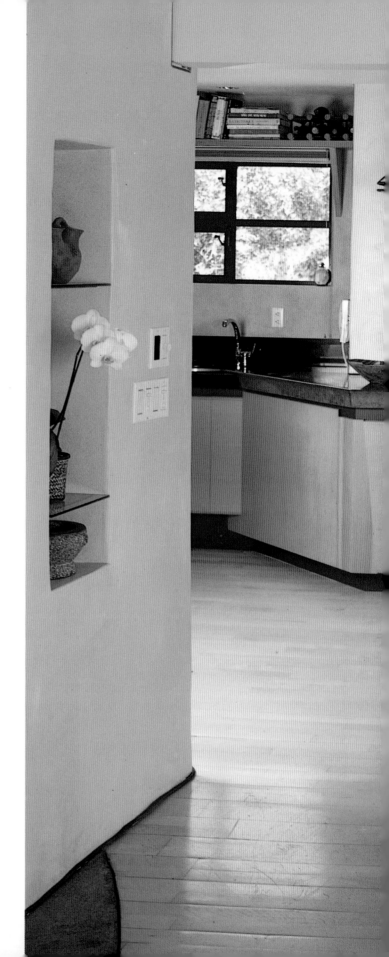

Beyond the work triangle

the work triangle was the invention of a group of researchers at Cornell University in the 1950s. Although it is a simplified approach to understanding kitchen design, the concept still has some value in planning today's more ambitious and versatile kitchens.

The triangle refers to the path formed by the arrangement of the sink, range, and refrigerator, the sum of whose sides, say the experts, should measure 12 to 22 feet. If the total walking distance is less than 12 feet, it means the work area in the kitchen is too cramped. If the distance is much greater than 22 feet, it means the key working parts of the kitchen are too far apart, resulting in undue walking and reaching on the part of the cook.

Today's ideal work triangle is more complex than that. For one thing, in many households, the kitchen often doubles as a family

Architect Travis Price created an unusual eight-sided island with cooktop, built-in storage, and polished granite surface to allow several people to work on meal preparation at the same time. It can be pressed into service as an elegant buffet for entertaining as well.

A custom-built counter
with a built-in pedestal
table creates a strong
visual separation of the
kitchen and the dining
area in a contemporary
house designed by architect
Mark McInturff. Careful
selection of materials
makes the open kitchen
compatible with the rest
of the house.

social center or home office. For another, there is often more than one cook to watch the pot. Finally, the work island, whether an antique chopping block or fancy new creation, is now as important to incorporate in a plan as the sink, range, and refrigerator.

The flexibility of the work triangle may be seen in the wide variety of today's successful kitchen layouts. Galley kitchens, cozy cottage kitchens, spacious open-plan kitchens, kitchens with peninsulas or islands ~ all can be made to function smoothly if the major elements of the room are properly deployed.

Other elements also contribute to the efficiency of a new or remodeled room. Lighting is often one of the cook's most neglected tools. Not only should it be brought to bear on every working surface, it should be exploited for the warmth it brings to a room. This includes overhead fixtures for ambience and under-cabinet strips to serve as task lighting.

Island workstations can be customized to suit any size room and fitted with cooktops, sinks, specialized surfaces, and storage to satisfy the most demanding cook.

Range hoods, providing important ventilation in a busy kitchen, are available in styles and materials that make them handsome architectural additions to the decor as well. And a new generation of built-in and compact appliances can be installed without intruding on the floor plan or calling undue attention to themselves. Custom cooktops and sinks bring both function and fashion to the kitchen.

With all these ingredients, today's kitchen performs more tasks than before, and does them better than ever.

In this kitchen barely bigger than a nook, key appliances are always just a step away, under a skylight installed to provide important illumination. Designer Eric Cohler put counters to good storage use, housing a small microwave oven and a variety of cooking utensils. Open shelves have been decoratively appointed instead of stocked with supplies.

Designer Heather Faulding devised this handsome center island, with its foot-long overhang on one side, to serve as a snack bar as well as a food preparation area (above). The dual-purpose island features a generous six-burner cooktop. Task lighting fits the room's traditional decor.

A country kitchen (opposite) takes advantage of the abundant natural light at the bay end of the house. Cabinets and appliances were installed to conform to the octagonal shape of the window. A movable butcher-block table provides additional storage and counter space.

The pass-through often functions as a convenient service counter in a galley kitchen where space is at a premium. Architect Frank Fitzgibbons chose overhead appliances, a built-in vent unit over the cooktop, and storage recesses that contribute to the clean-lined interior. White painted surfaces help to make the room seem larger than it is.

Architects Kenneth Garcia and Jan Abell, along with designer Davis Mackiernan, created a compact work triangle in this U-shaped kitchen. The refrigerator is located where its frequent use won't interfere with other tasks. Sconces and under-cabinet strips provide ambient lighting; a skylight does the rest.

In the remodeled loft of author Lee Bailey, all appliances are compactly and efficiently located on one wall. For ultimate entertaining flexibility, the owner designed a pair of marble-topped dining room tables on wheels. Joined together, the tables can accommodate a crowd. Apart, one seats six for dinner while the other, rolled against a wall, serves as a sideboard. An island of carpeting, along with movable wall panels, helps delineate an otherwise cavernous space.

A masterful host, Bailey pays as much attention to lighting as any other design element in the kitchen. All fixtures are on a dimmer system, "up for cocktail chatter, down for dinner table conversation."

Designer Beverly Ellsley used three kinds of lighting to help increase this kitchen's serviceability: under-cabinet strips, mounted as far forward as possible, for counter work; ceiling-mounted track lighting to brighten the entire room, especially otherwise dark recesses between the cabinets and high ceiling; and two glass hanging fixtures to illuminate the island work surface and enhance the decor. The white-faced ovens (left) blend in with the custom cabinetry. Most appliance manufacturers offer a choice of colors and options for customizing their products to the style of the individual kitchen.

In a fanciful kitchen by designer Agnes Bourne, a commercial range has its own cutting board and six gas burners under a custom vent hood with built-in lighting. The butcher-block island features a double stainless-steel sink, a side drainboard, and a sleek single-lever faucet.

Designer Beverly Ellsley's
two-story addition to an
updated Victorian house
includes a kitchen opening
out from the porch-
like family room. The
U-shaped counter encloses
the work area without
turning its back on the
social goings-on. New
kitchen cabinets with
recessed panels, glass-
paned doors, and bracket
feet are in keeping with
the old-fashioned mood
of the house.

A small kitchen designed
by architect Mark Simon
overlooks the dining area
from behind its elegant
work counter; the layout
keeps the nuts and bolts
of meal preparation out
of sight. French doors
allow natural light to
flood the kitchen by day.
For entertaining, lamps
on overhead cross-ties
illuminate the room
through panels of silk.

chapter 5

STORAGE SOLUTIONS

Kitchens have come a long way since the American home first began to enjoy the fruits of modernity. With electrification and the "appliance age," the kitchen probably went through the most dramatic metamorphosis of all the rooms in the house. As the homemaker's domain, it became a beehive of activities, from the daily cycle of meal preparation to canning and preserving and holiday baking. And as it became busier and bigger, and more and more tools, equipment, and supplies developed, the need for efficient and handy storage became critical.

Introduced in the early part of this century, the Hoosier cabinet was the original all-in-one workstation, the homemaker's answer to the problem of organizing and storing her growing pantry and batterie de cuisine. Today, there are many sophisticated and ingenious solutions for stowing and stashing all kinds of gear in kitchens of all shapes and sizes. Fitted drawers, pull-out bins, and customized cabinet interiors exploit all the under-counter space previously designated as no-man's-land. Cabinets with adjustable shelves and doors outfitted with spice racks and sliding mini-pantries allow maximum exploitation of a kitchen's above-counter storage capacity. Open shelves and freestanding shelving systems take up the rest of the burden. Along with fresh new approaches to furnishing this all-important room, there are now creative storage solutions to suit every budget and taste.

Lessons in design

a well-designed kitchen with adequate provision for precious storage is not the product of luck or happenstance. The San Francisco-based cooking teacher and restaurant consultant whose kitchen is profiled here did a lot of soul-searching and note-taking before she started a major kitchen renovation. For three years, she kept a record of her family's traffic patterns, charted how she herself used her work areas and moved back and forth between them, and recorded the frequency with which she used her appliances and utensils. By the time she had hired a contractor, she knew her preferences and needs inside and out.

Because this homeowner gives cooking classes for as many as 25 students at a time, it was vital that the kitchen be able to handle a crowd. She also was determined to avoid trendy or whimsical features that might inter-

The cookbook nook was designed to house a cooking professional's 700-volume collection; at the same time it gives the kitchen, complete with its own fireplace, the tranquil air of a study. Rosy polished-granite counters, bleached and painted red oak cabinets, and white limestone floors bathe the room in warm, honey tones.

77

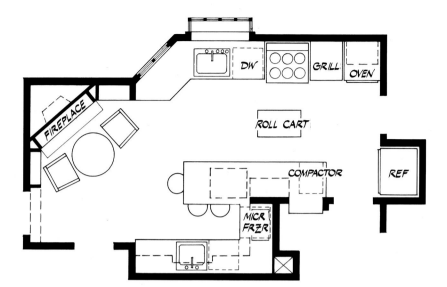

Increasing storage was this homeowner's first priority (opposite, clockwise from top right): A compartment for food-wrap dispensers slides out from under the counter; fifteen-inch-deep drawers keep gadgets at the ready; a segmented bin under the charbroiler eliminates the hunt-and-peck system for locating pot lids; the trash compactor is conveniently situated below a cutting-board surface.

fere with the long-term needs of this very practical room. "There's nothing at all gimmicky about it," she says of the resulting kitchen, which is nearly 300 square feet.

By eliminating a wall between kitchen and pantry and replacing it with a peninsula workstation, two distinct areas were created, one for food preparation and cooking, the other for cleanup. In the first, easy access to cooking utensils and equipment was a major consideration. Pots and pans had to be within "grabbing" distance of the range. Hanging them from bars attached to the hood of the stove proved to be an effective solution. Compartmentalized bins were installed wherever possible to increase storage and convenience. A gleaming collection of copper pots hang from a rack above the peninsula, along with a multitude of strainers.

Additional storage abounds. Under the counter, more drawers replace cabinet doors, including one designed to store spice jars so their labels can be easily read and another that pulls out to dispense food wrap. A butch-

er-block cart, complete with storage for knives and food processor equipment, can be wheeled around the room to provide another handy surface wherever needed. Glass fronts for both refrigerator and wall-hung cabinets allow the cook and her pupils to find what they need in a hurry. Honey tones and natural materials soften the room's functional edge. Sponge-painted walls, in varying shades of buff, result in a glare-free surface, and rosy polished granite adds high-performance elegance to the countertops and backsplashes. The unusual white limestone floor is more durable than vinyl or wood and "feels like velvet" underfoot.

Utilitarian details and luxurious finishing materials notwithstanding, the crowning glory of this very personal kitchen is a library for the owner's vast collection of cookbooks. At the last minute the owner decided that installing an old-fashioned brick oven in the kitchen would be impractical. In its place are the floor-to-ceiling bookshelves flanking a wood-burning fireplace.

Overhead racks ~ one for
all-purpose pots and the
other for copper cookware
and strainers ~ and a
work island on wheels
bring this large kitchen to
the cook's fingertips (left).
Above the cooktop, an
open shelf holds the
most frequently used
utensils in crocks.

Two sinks and two
dishwashers accelerate
the cleanup effort when
cooking classes are held.
Glass-paned doors were
chosen for the cabinets
to make it easy to find
tableware and serving
pieces (above).

81

Everything old is new again

a new kitchen with the comforting feel of an old general store and the serviceability of a well-organized keeping room demonstrates an unconventional but successful approach to the problem of storage. For this kitchen's primary user, the surprising solution to cabinet storage was to have no cabinets at all. "The client was quite specific about not wanting any cabinetry or shelves in the room," says Gene Reed, an antiques dealer who worked in collaboration with the client to create a kitchen appropriate to a newly built salt-box colonial.

Instead of turning to standard wall-hung and base cabinets for solving the problem of where to put things, the owner's prized collection of painted cupboards and chests was tapped to furnish the room. "We worked as sensibly as we could, given this rather unorthodox approach," says Reed. With a combination of paneled doors, glass doors, drawers, and shelves, the pieces ~ including a nineteenth-century apothecary-store fixture and an elegant Irish linen press ~ provide more than adequate storage space. They also allow the owner to showcase her collections of stoneware and crockery and to stash sets of china, glassware, and table linens.

Designed as an open space with enough room to accommodate a large seating area in front of the hearth, the kitchen takes advantage of its open wall areas to show off other unusual finds. A striking collection of decora-

A painted cupboard with raised-panel doors houses everything from prized pottery to daily dishware (above).

Old Shaker boxes, apothecary jars with domed lids, and a double-decker spice box provide plenty of room for odds and ends (opposite). Overhead, rafters display the weaving skills of early settlers and Native Americans.

83

tive signs features a carved and painted one from a Pennsylvania general store and an English reversed-glass butcher's sign.

Small antiques ~ boxes, baskets, bowls, and jars ~ also figure prominently in the organization of the room, both for their visual appeal and for their suitability as holders of cutlery, candles, napkins, staples, recipes, small utensils, and all manner of culinary paraphernalia.

"This kitchen wasn't 'designed' so much as it was improvised, using what we had, some new pieces, and moving things around until they fit," explains Reed. "We didn't set out to find a cupboard for a wall here and a table for a corner over there."

As a result, all but unnoticed in the room are the modern conveniences. The dishwasher, stove, ovens, and refrigerator all take a back seat to the old-time furnishings. That's why the room looks and feels like a moment out of the past.

The spectacular apothecary chest, with its 49 drawers, keeps small possessions perfectly organized but always at hand. An Irish pine linen press has the deep shelves and drawers suitable for storing multiple sets of china, tablecloths, napkins, and place mats. Dining accommodations in front of the hearth consist of a newly made table and bent-willow chairs and an old rustic settee.

Wall-to-wall storage

t he walk-in pantry, the dream storage solution for any kitchen, is not a realistic option in most houses, but today there are many practical and imaginative alternatives to keeping the kitchen workplace well stocked and organized for action, and keeping work counters clear. Cabinetry, shelving, and other systems using peg racks, pot racks, and hooks are available in such a wide variety of shapes, finishes, and price ranges that they are flexible enough to solve storage problems in kitchens of every kind.

Wall-hung cabinets, whether standard-issue or custom-built, have the advantage of providing great volumes of storage area without intruding on the room's basic floor plan. Those that are ceiling height provide maximum storage space and are especially effective in apartment kitchens. The overhead space created by cabinetry that doesn't reach the ceiling can be used to store or display large serving pieces, baskets, and the like. Cabinets fronted with glass doors are ideal for the cook who likes to see everything at a glance or show off colorful china and dishware. Solid doors or glass doors backed with panels of fabric might be the better choice for cooks who prefer to keep their "pantry" out of sight.

Base cabinets have become a great new source for storage. Drawers of varying depths and fitted with specialized dividers and compartments hold everything from spices and table linens to the array of small utensils and

Huge antique pieces such as the pilastered pine shelving and the multi-drawer counter salvaged from an old dry-goods store give a kitchen instant storage (below).

A country kitchen enlists rustic elements to keep everything in its place (opposite). Hooks on the exposed beam store a set of cast-iron skillets. Open shelves holding a collection of bowls provide both storage and decoration. Old crocks with new wooden lids hold the baker's staples.

The brass crossbar on the hood of a professional chef's stove in designer Tricia Guild's kitchen offers the luxury of space for keeping multiple implements, including soup ladles, readily at hand. Recessed open shelving keeps kitchenware at the cook's fingertips without taking space away from the counters. In this alcove, crocks, cruets, and home-canned fruits and olives play a decorative as well as utilitarian role.

tools used in daily food preparation. Roll-out bins make it easy to retrieve large pots and pans, mixing bowls, and small appliances.

Adjustable shelving systems bring a high degree of efficiency to the kitchen, whether installed inside cabinets or used independently on walls, often turning otherwise wasted nooks and crannies into serviceable space.

In a break from the recent past, when kitchens were uniform in character and typified by unbroken rows of cabinets, today's "unfitted" look takes advantage of the practical and decorative virtues of traditional furniture borrowed from other rooms in the house. Old cupboards and hutches have made an amiable return to the modern kitchen, pro-

viding storage but also infusing the room with warmth and personality. Other pieces with storage capacities include linen presses, dressers, and even furniture recycled from old apothecaries, dry-goods stores, and other emporia from another time.

Finally, today's innovative kitchen makes use of a vast selection of small containers, charming to look at, to play myriad important storage roles in and around the cook's corner. Baskets, boxes, crocks, mason jars, and countless other kinds of containers come in handy for holding just about anything of a certain size. They can be found at auction, in flea markets, or even up in the attic. All it takes is a bit of imagination.

A floor-to-ceiling pantry
for table linens and wet
bar in architect Robert
Kleinschmidt's apartment
shows how careful plan-
ning and organization
can maximize the capacity
of closet spaces (above).

A wheeled cabinet with
drawers on two sides con-
veniently rolls under a
counter when not in
service (top right).

In the space under a cooktop, doors were replaced
with drawers for easier
access to often-used small
utensils and spices (right).
Potholders and cutting
boards are stowed in
the open recesses directly
below the cooktop.

Glass-paned doors give a
china-closet appearance
to the wall-hung cabinets
in this New England
kitchen (below).
Otherwise wasted space
between the cabinets and
the countertops is put to
use with the installation
of a shallow shelf.

Wall-hung cabinets of
hand-rubbed bird's-eye
maple provide elegant
kitchen storage in designer Linda Banks's kitchen
(opposite). With their
raised panels and hand-
carved wood pulls, the
base cabinets also resem-
ble fine furniture.

The walk-in pantry offers the convenience of keeping all household wares and equipment in the open (right). Innovative conversions of closets adjacent to kitchens feature floor-to-ceiling adjustable shelving, as well as deep drawers for holding linens and place mats.

Architect Jamie Wollens created an old-fashioned-looking cabinet for this loft kitchen with the aid of a glass-paned door he found on a city street (below right). The glass shelves add to the modern look of the room.

A newly built pantry with a mullioned glass front by architect Mark Mascheroni (opposite) aims to show off as well as store favorite china, crystal, and serving pieces.

The galley kitchens found in many city dwellings demand creative storage solutions. In this sleek version, designers Peter Shelton and Lee Mindel used recessed overhead cabinets and a custom configuration of both shallow and deep drawers and cabinets below the work surface.

Architect Robert Kleinschmidt remodeled his apartment kitchen to "work like a machine."

The room features a countertop of solid-surfacing material with a pull-out cutting board

and streamlined cabinetry that contains more than the eye ever sees.

The stainless-steel work center in a country kitchen designed by William Diamond and Anthony Baratta is equipped with a full complement of drawers as well as a built-in dishwasher and a second sink (opposite). The kitchen's entire battery of pots and pans is stored on the overhead rack.

The principal work counter from a turn-of-the-century butcher's shop finds a new home as the focal point in a kitchen with old-fashioned tastes (above left). Its deep drawers pull out from either side, an ingenious practical feature designer Carol Zimmerman couldn't resist.

Borrowing from hard-working kitchens in the south of France, designer Paul Bailly used wicker baskets as drawers, easily removed from built-in niches (above right). Baskets hold napkins, potholders, place mats, cutting boards, and even cooking staples.

Adjustable shelving has evolved into a sophisticated range of choices since it was first introduced. A freestanding stainless-steel floor-to-ceiling unit in Tricia Guild's kitchen offers more customized storage space than many good-size cupboards (above).

Architects Barbara Weinstein and Jeffrey Milstein devised this solution to a bare-walled kitchen (opposite top). It requires nothing more than metal brackets and wood boards cut to order to create a place to put away china and serving pieces.

Designer Lyn Peterson used a wire grid suspended from the ceiling over a counter to hold bowls and baskets on top and serve as a handy rack for pots and tools below (opposite below). The shelves extend over the stovetop to take full advantage of the wall space.

chapter 6

SURFACES AND FINISHES

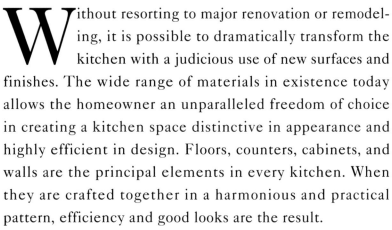

Without resorting to major renovation or remodeling, it is possible to dramatically transform the kitchen with a judicious use of new surfaces and finishes. The wide range of materials in existence today allows the homeowner an unparalleled freedom of choice in creating a kitchen space distinctive in appearance and highly efficient in design. Floors, counters, cabinets, and walls are the principal elements in every kitchen. When they are crafted together in a harmonious and practical pattern, efficiency and good looks are the result.

Repainting or repapering the walls is always a good starting point for change; do-it-yourselfers can often complete the job in a single weekend. Flooring and countertops usually pose more elaborate challenges for the remodeler, but the effort is worth it, as these utilitarian surfaces make the most impact on the daily life of the kitchen. Cabinets and other storage components lend themselves to a surprising variety of rehab possibilities, from as simple a change as replacing hardware to a full-scale refacing using laminates, new glass doors, stains or paint. The materials chosen for walls, floors, countertops, and cabinet fronts range across the spectrum of color, finish, and texture, and ultimately have a far-reaching effect on both the practicality and aesthetics of every kitchen.

From bleak house
to chic house

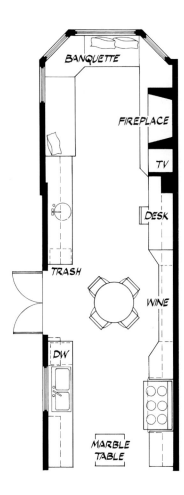

A granite-topped pedestal table effectively divides the long kitchen into two areas, one for food preparation and one for dining and socializing (opposite). The custom-made wine rack provides a pleasing break on a 40-foot-long wall.

a variety of classic materials and finishes proved to be the key in helping designer Daen Scheiber solve the unique challenge of remodeling a long, narrow kitchen in a four-story San Francisco house dating from 1902. The room measures 40 feet long but only 11 feet wide, so the primary challenge was to avoid a bowling-alley look. At the same time, says the designer, "The clients wanted modern conveniences, but they didn't want the kitchen to look more modern than the Edwardian-era house it was in."

A previous owner had updated the kitchen in the 1970s, adding butcher-block counters and tile floors, but the present owners found the space dark and unwelcoming, woefully short on storage, and lacking any distinguishing architectural characteristics.

By breaking the space into clearly defined zones and by introducing handcrafted details and a range of color finishes, Scheiber created a utilitarian kitchen plan with all the work areas, living space, and storage the family needed, but one that made for an inviting and homey setting as well. Drawers and cabinets were tailored to fit every tool and utensil in the cook's batterie de cuisine. A toaster and microwave oven were built into cabinets near the dining table. The designer also created a visually arresting wine rack as an adjunct to the basement wine cellar.

What makes the kitchen as attractive as it is functional is the selection of materials for the room's surfaces, and the choice of a variety of both complementary and contrasting finishes. Raised paneling on the oak cabinets conveys the immediate impression of hand-crafted furniture, and the addition of crown molding to the upper casework heightens the effect. A teal tint added to the whitewash gives the wood an antique look and breaks the monotony that might otherwise exist in a room with so much wood surface.

Pink granite lends a turn-of-the-century character to the countertops. The polished surface, apart from being practical for kitchen chores, provides an elegant contrast to the stainless steel of the appliances and pewter of the vintage armchairs around the dining area table. And all the reflective surfaces contribute to the room's sunny atmosphere.

Limestone-tile backsplashes were chosen to finish off the counters. With its diamond-shaped granite insets, this surface offsets the room's solid surfaces with pattern and texture.

The front end of the room, with sink, dishwasher, and an antique baker's table, is the food preparation area. The back end of the room, with the granite-topped table, a counter that becomes a coffee bar for parties, and a window banquette, is the dining and entertaining sphere. Under the banquette is storage for the board games frequently played in the adjoining family room.

If proof was needed as to the redesign's effectiveness, two parties given immediately following the renovation provided it. The kitchen was the pivotal room for each gathering and handled nearly 150 guests on each occasion without a hitch.

A built-in granite-topped desk with file storage creates precious space for family paperwork.

A commercial range, its sidewalls insulated for residential use, fits safely between kitchen cabinets.

Hardwood planks replaced Mexican tile on the kitchen floor, adding warmth and reducing the noise level. A pass-through at the sink, a pair of glass doors opening onto the side yard, and a large arched window help make a very narrow room seem more spacious. An antique baker's table and a set of 1920s pewter armchairs invest the room with vintage character.

Satisfying the visual appetite

using the classic surface materials of the Mediterranean kitchen for inspiration, a San Francisco designer collapsed a series of small rooms into one space to create "a kind of cooking piazza reflecting two hundred years of tradition."

The house in which Agnes Bourne's ambitious renovation occurred had been built in the 1920s in the grand style of an eighteenth-century French manor house, so it started out with interesting architectural elements. The kitchen, however, was a cramped space that had been disastrously redone in the early 1960s, its harvest gold and orange scheme quickly becoming outdated.

Retaining the handsome transom windows and a remarkable copper vent hood from the original house, the designer left no other sur-

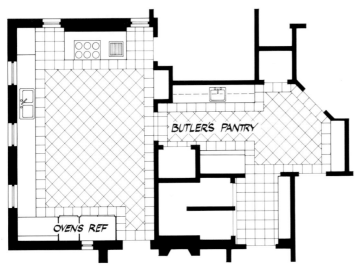

Cabinets banked on one wall create the effect of an old-fashioned armoire (above).

Hand-forged iron tables topped with both marble and butcher block, from the designer's furniture collection, provide the cook with versatile work surfaces (opposite). A foliage motif, both real and crafted on the tables, adds a naturalistic note.

107

face untouched in her effort to enrich the room with a warm patina that evokes a sense of the past. She used large terracotta pavers, salvaged from an actual chateau in France, for the new floor. New handmade French tiles were used to surface the counters and the work area under the copper hood. "The idea was to create a cooking hearth like one found in an eighteenth-century house in France or Italy," says Bourne. "I also liked being able to bring the antique tiles together with newly made tiles that happened to come from the same area in France."

A new floor plan encompassing nearly 1,000 square feet gives visitors the impression "of walking down a little alley" as they proceed through the service pantry to the kitchen. "A kitchen, to me, is the center of life in the house, a public space where everyone comes together," the designer explains. "The bigger

An "information niche," built as the command center for an on-the-go cook, houses a TV and small desktop area (above left).

The beauty of handmade tile lies in their irregular coloration (above right). The large open space under the cooktop was designed to resemble a wood-burning hearth.

The surprising color of the faucet and lamp necks overhead adds "a dash of paprika" to the Mediterranean stew of design elements (opposite). Wall frescoes portray beguiling images of an old-world countryside.

the kitchen, the better ~ although I do like small ones, too, the friendly kind where cooks bump into each other."

Bourne called in skilled artisans for the room's traditional finishing touches. Instead of simply covering the old dark walnut cabinets of the original kitchen with a fresh coat of paint, new doors and drawers were installed, then hand-stained a soft turquoise.

In a more elaborate embellishment, the moldings and surrounds of all the windows in the room were painted with a faux finish to resemble the stone that might be found in a centuries-old villa in the Italian countryside.

For the pièce de résistance, Bourne commissioned a series of wall frescoes depicting pastoral scenes. The beautifully executed landscapes and ethereal skies of the paintings lend a timeless quality to the room.

"I wanted the soft, earthy colors of a Mediterranean palette to predominate," says the designer. "It's a luscious kitchen designed to fulfill one's visual appetite. Looking out from the room, surrounded by its murals, with gardens in the foreground and the tiled roofline of a neighboring house in the distance, you almost think you're in Tuscany or the south of France."

A working service pantry, dedicated to cleanup and serving tasks, is also a passageway to the rest of the house, so its surfaces have been finished with as much attention as those found in the kitchen.

Designer Agnes Bourne chose decorative limestone tile set in a harlequin pattern on the wall for a picturesque effect (above). Translucent glass bricks were used instead of clear glass to conceal an unsightly view without losing natural light.

A combination of painting techniques ~ dry-brushing, sponging, and rubbing ~ gives the wood cabinets the look of stone and the ceiling the look of lofty clouds (opposite). Mirrored backsplashes add light and drama to the room.

On the face of it

r ather than just serving as bland platforms, floors are the new welcome mats in the kitchen. Wood floors can be painted, pickled, polished, or left plain. For a completely different look and feel, ceramic or terracotta tiles, glazed or unglazed, are available in a wide variety of colors and shapes. Then there is vinyl. The resilient flooring of today bears no resemblance to the linoleum of yesteryear; it is easy to install and maintain and comes in colors and patterns to suit every style. Still other floor choices for the kitchen include slate, stone, and brick.

Counters are the kitchen's battlefields, submitted to the greatest wear and tear and expected to perform and endure. Available materials range from high-pressure laminates that are as easy on the eye as on the budget, to the indestructible and hygienic stainless-steel borrowed from restaurants, to elegant materials imbued with old-world patina such as granite and marble. Other choices include wood, ceramic tile, slate, solid-surfacing materials, and even poured and molded concrete.

Counter backsplashes serve the useful purpose of protecting the kitchen wall from moisture, but they also add an extra design element to a room. Tiles set in interesting patterns or custom-painted ~ even mirrored surfaces ~ lend a colorful presence to this sometimes neglected area under the cabinets.

Cabinets can receive a new lease on life simply by having their doors refinished or

replaced. Wood veneer and laminates are attractive alternatives to more expensive solid wood for cabinets. Paints, lacquers, stains, bleaches, and color washes are other effective ways to transform wood cabinets.

Two coats of gloss or semi-gloss enamel paint are usually recommended for walls, providing an easy-to-clean surface in a room where spills and stains are occupational hazards. Flat oil or latex paint works best on most ceilings. When it comes to wallpaper, vinyl is more practical than paper because it stands up to repeated washings.

More elaborate custom-finishing techniques can add dramatic decorative texture to surfaces: Combing is the application of paint with a cardboard tool with comb-like teeth. Dry-brushing embellishes a base coat of paint with the feathery strokes of an almost dry brush that has a small amount of another color paint on it. In sponging, paint is applied to a wall or cabinet with a sponge, so that a pebbled finish is

achieved. Stippling creates a similar effect, with the use of a blunt, bristled brush. In texturing, a glaze coat of paint is added to the base coat with crumpled newspaper or a rag. Faux finishes are the most exacting surface treatments available and require the hand of a skilled artisan to transform ordinary wood into surfaces that resemble elegant wood or stone.

Wood cabinets, pickled cedar paneling, and a butcher-block countertop bring texture to a monochromatic kitchen by architect Stephen Muse (above left). In a loft kitchen by Michael Rubin, the translucent glass of the screens and cabinet doors is an airy alternative to solid surfaces (above right).

In a keeping room enlivened by a rich assortment of antique furnishings, the patina of old wood shines through. A butcher's chopping block can do double duty as a serving table; an old cupboard lends its stately presence and storage capacity to the room. The stone hearth and solid plank floor are time-worn surfaces that only get better with age.

The choice of pomegranate
red for the walls provides
a blazing backdrop
for the natural wood
surfaces of the harvest
table, the custom work
island, and a pair
of weathered window
shutters brought inside
for use as cabinet doors
(above and left). The
chimney wall is made
of Vermont stone.

In a country kitchen dominated by wood beams, cabinets, and open shelving, designer Dan Carithers chose hand-painted Portuguese ceramic tile and durable terracotta tile flooring to inject colorful relief in the rustic room (above). Off-white walls crisply define the kitchen's parameters.

French doors in designer Linda Banks's small kitchen provide natural light, which is reflected in a variety of surfaces and finishes: stainless-steel counter and vent hood, white tile on the walls, and a polished hardwood floor. Shiny copper utensils provide the finishing touches.

A Scandinavian pine
hutch, wall-hung spice
rack, and dining table
and chairs mix happily
with sleek laminate
cabinets and counters,
supplying texture as well
as color to a family room.
Designer Lyn Peterson
added terracotta floor
tiles and a grid-patterned
vinyl fabric to the walls
and vaulted ceiling for
even more visual interest.

Architect Walter Chatham created this chic post-industrial look in a Florida townhouse with poured-concrete counters, tile floors and walls, and stainless-steel appliances. Another wall, sponged with gunmetal-silver paint, and a set of newly made metal chairs with a retro flair, complete the high-tech look.

Designer Beverly Ellsley faux-finished the smooth surfaces and raised panels of these cabinets to resemble two varieties of marble (above left). The countertop and backsplash sport hand-painted ceramic tile in a floral pattern topped by a leafy border.

The striped blue-and-white wallpaper in this small kitchen designed by Sue Westphal draws the eye upward, helping to make the room feel bigger (above right). The ceramic wall mural and the island tiles are all hand-painted.

To provide softness in this tiled kitchen, designer Florence Perchuk introduced graceful curves in the festive tile wreath between the stovetop and vent, and in the delicate iron and wood-slat chairs (bottom right).

chapter 7

DECORATIVE TOUCHES

Once the working kitchen is in place, the designer in all of us can go to work. Decorating, in its broadest sense, is all the creative finishing touches brought to a room. In the case of the kitchen, it's the use of color, pattern, fabric, and furnishings to achieve a personal style that also fits in with the rest of the home.

Many kitchen looks are homegrown in nature, rooted in strong regional traditions. The planked floors and painted cupboards of New England are in striking contrast to the adobe walls and viga beams of the Southwest. Some kitchens derive their character from the architectural form of the house. A Georgian townhouse with high ceilings and towering windows may boast a stately kitchen worthy of Jeeves the butler, while a cottage or bungalow with its humbler dimensions is likely to have a cozy, dollhouse-size space.

Kitchen decor can be formal or casual, ultramodern or old-fashioned, clean or cluttered, depending on taste. Color is far and away the most direct way to transform a room quickly; wallpaper, fabric, and even scatter rugs are excellent ways to introduce it in a kitchen. Furnishings, whether an antique pine dry sink or an upholstered slipper chair, add warmth and serve a purpose, too. Finally, the cook's favorite things ~ collections of baskets, books, bottles, or bibelots ~ help to stamp the kitchen with a decorating signature all its own.

Letting the sunshine in

a neglected kitchen in a back room of a Boston townhouse built in 1824 has been vividly brought to life, without losing a bit of its antique charm, with a little imagination and a great deal of style.

The challenge for the design team Arrel Linderman and Sudie Schenck was to create a warm, livable space out of a room that had last been updated four decades before. A high ceiling, three east-facing windows, and a massive wood-burning stove were the dominant features in the old kitchen; and generous built-in cabinets and cupboards were original furnishings, all well worth preserving or incorporating into the remodel.

The major structural change the designers imposed was enlarging the existing windows, permitting more light to enter and providing

Surprising kitchen seating, these elegant slipper chairs and sofa are upholstered in an exotic English floral chintz, with a wear-proof dark background. Mixed in with modern appliances and a professional gas range, antiques and family heirlooms endow this Beacon Hill kitchen with nineteenth-century elegance.

125

a view of a newly planted courtyard garden complete with fountain and espaliered hydrangea. This, combined with a bright yellow paint on the walls, transformed a dreary interior into a much sunnier place.

The old brown linoleum floor was ripped up and replaced with vinyl tile in a classic checkerboard pattern. "We didn't want anything to seem glitzy or new," Linderman explains. "The black-and-white design of the floor fits in with the old-fashioned character of the house and is a striking contrast to the yellow walls."

Even though both owners, husband and wife, are avid amateur chefs, a conscious decision was made to limit counter space in order to prevent the room from becoming "too kitcheny." Instead, a rustic farm table was brought in, which serves both as a work surface and dining table.

The room was thoroughly updated with commercial appliances, but it surrenders none of its original vintage qualities. Old French candlesticks, made into table lamps, cast a comforting glow. A tin storage bin from the couple's summer house does duty as a side table. Even the venerable Cyrus Carpenter stove, a faithful family retainer from way back, has survived as a showcase for some of the family's other prized possessions.

Bedecked with hurricane lamps, Staffordshire spaniels, and a red tole coal bucket, the massive cast-iron stove fuels the homeowners' passion for antiques (top).

French park seats and a Victorian plant stand, used for storing cookbooks, have been appropriated from the garden for unexpectedly useful service in the kitchen (above).

A marbleized vinyl floor was laid out on the diagonal to make uneven walls appear straight (opposite). The sunny yellow walls maximize the natural light that pours in through east-facing windows.

A thoroughly modern Victorian

a n 1884 carriage house with eight gables and a fanciful turret didn't lack for exterior decoration, but a series of bland remodelings had left its interiors badly in need of attention.

The kitchen, a leftover from a 1950s remodeling, was a tiny, cramped galley. But an adjacent 22-by-22-foot utility room offered a solution: By gutting the old kitchen and removing the wall separating it from the utility room, designer and homeowner Connie Beale was able to carve a multipurpose 450-square-foot space out of the increased floor area.

In planning the decor of the kitchen, Beale took her cues from the architectural style of the house, which was distinctly Victorian. "I knew I wanted our design to reflect the period in which the carriage house was built, as part of a great estate, but I didn't want it to look like a period statement," she says.

To complement the original sets of mullioned windows high on one wall of the kitchen, Beale installed a pair of French doors to capture morning light and provide a view of the heart-shaped perennial flower garden. Cabinets were built on site by a carpenter, just as they would have been at the turn of the century, to take full advantage of the space available in a room with 10-foot ceilings. Curved brackets under the cabinets and curved shelves on the built-in hutch are special craftsman touches.

Other custom features include a roll-out pastry counter, shallow drawers for storing linens, and a handy spice rack installed on the back of a cabinet door.

Period light fixtures, pottery collections, handmade dhurrie rugs, and carpenter-built battenboard cabinets and cupboard are some of the accents that give the kitchen the prettiness of a living room (opposite).

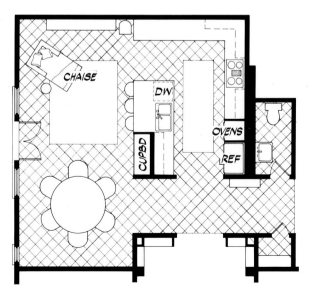

The modern, low-maintenance work surfaces resist an image of sterility thanks to their Victorian color palette. The tile backsplash is reminiscent of pewter, the tile floor is the shade of old copper pots, and the solid-surface countertops convey the impression of marble. Collections of the designer's favorite pottery, folk art, and antiques provide the finishing touches. "We wanted the kitchen to function as a traditional work center," Beale says, "but also to be pretty as a picture."

A pair of decorative glass doors expands the dining area onto the terrace in warm months. Natural linen curtains frame the lovely view (above).

The addition of an old shopkeeper's chest of many drawers and a new wicker chaise longue draped in patchwork and plumped with pillows offers interest, warmth, and comfort (left).

Little things mean a lot

d ecorative details can make all the difference in the look of a kitchen: A painted rustic table and a collection of old birdhouses bring the country into a city apartment; a series of contemporary black-and-white photographs lends an urbane dimension to a rustic scullery in the woods.

Commercial kitchens are sterile-looking because they have to be, but the home kitchen, answering to only the most personal of rule books, can take on any personality. It can be as plain and unassuming as apple pie, as spicy and surprising as an exotic stew. The kitchen tends to decorate itself. Cookbooks, crockery, utensils, fruits, and vegetables all contribute color and texture at the same time they are fulfilling their humble purposes.

Sometimes, details seem to almost magically transform the room. A brand-new kitchen ages gracefully in no time when antiques and folk pieces become part of the decor. A tired but serviceable room from an earlier decade receives a new lease on life with a fresh paint job, a surprising floor treatment, or new wallpaper. Knobs, fittings, and fixtures can be changed with little effort and expense, resulting in a significant improvement in the look of the room. Bracketed shelves, plate and pot racks, and containers of all kinds can be put to good decorative use. Framed family photos or diminutive paintings improve a blank wall or empty shelf in a way that utilitarian objects often can't.

A plate rack and wood and wicker baskets are put to good use in this kitchen designed by Julie Atwood, at the same time lending their rustic charm to the work area (above). A painted niche under the counter is an unexpected perch for a prized basket. Mediterranean colors *infuse the room with a warm, welcoming atmosphere (opposite). Pretty pots of herbs and flowers thrive on every available surface. A linen shade frames the window, and colored grout around the tiles creates a pleasing pattern on the counter.*

An eighteenth-century farmhouse kitchen, its uneven stone walls painted white, is fitted out with a collection of market baskets, plain pine cupboards, and hand-crafted chestnut chairs with woven seats. The neutral color scheme is a wonderful backdrop for the unvarnished country look.

Designer Jorge Letelier used rugs to add pattern and color and help to muffle the clatter of cooking in his kitchen (above left). The wrought-iron towel holder with a rooster motif graces the door with barnyard charm.

Plates in a painted cupboard show off their designs even when not in use (above right). Recycled mustard crocks make perfect holders for bone-handled cutlery and other items easily lost track of in drawers. The terracotta flower pots, painted white, add their diminutive appeal and demonstrate the decorating potential of even the smallest objects.

The kitchen of a 1922 Craftsman-style cottage in California remains true to its roots with frilly café curtains, vintage table linens, antique wicker chairs, and a checkerboard vinyl floor (above). The hanging light fixture and the crystal drawer and cabinet pulls are old-fashioned accessories. Other colorful touches, including pottery bowls full of seasonal bounty, reveal this is the kitchen of a working gardener. Floral patterns and the color red, so prevalent here, are also found throughout the rest of the house, which the owner conceived of as "one big playhouse."

In the kitchen, antiques,
large or small, always
make a good impression,
lending their character
and charm to what other-
wise could be a sterile
interior. Where space is at
a premium, vintage pieces
should be made to serve
practical purposes, too.
Designer Karin Blake
used an old jelly cupboard
to keep colorful dishware
out in the open (top left).
Serving pitchers make
convenient containers for
casual flower displays
(above). A wooden dough
bowl or a primitive
painted box provide
storage both for necessities
and luxuries (below left).

Fabric, used wisely, can transform an ordinary kitchen into a special room. Here, designer Florence Perchuk replaced conventional base-cabinet doors with a cheery plaid. A sash of elegant fabric lined with stripes adds a touch of softness to a bare window; stripes reappear on the pantry doors.

Unique furnishings in the same kitchen create an old-world atmosphere, from the French marble-topped table and the antique metal chairs to the old metal pot stand and tin sconce filled with sheaves of wheat. The classic black-and-white vinyl tile floor completes the Gallic mood.

139

DIRECTORY OF DESIGNERS AND ARCHITECTS

Jan Abell
Tampa, Florida

Julie Atwood
San Rafael, California

Paul Bailly
Los Angeles, California

Linda Banks
Norwalk, Connecticut

Anthony Baratta
New York, New York

Connie Beale
Greenwich, Connecticut

Kathryn McGraw Berry
New York, New York

Karin Blake
Malibu, California

Agnes Bourne
San Francisco, California

Dan Carithers
Atlanta, Georgia

Walter Chatham
New York, New York

Fu-Tung Cheng
Berkeley, California

Eric Cohler
New York, New York

Carl D'Aquino
New York, New York

William Diamond
New York, New York

Beverly Ellsley
Westport, Connecticut

Heather Faulding
New York, New York

J. Frank Fitzgibbons
Los Angeles, California

Ted Flato
San Antonio, Texas

Kenneth Garcia
Tampa, Florida

Tricia Guild
London, England

Robert Kleinschmidt
Chicago, Illinois

Jorge Letelier
New York, New York

Arrel Linderman
Boston, Massachusetts

Davis Mackiernan
New York, New York

Mark Mascheroni
New York, New York

Mark McInturff
Washington, D.C.

Jeffrey Milstein
Woodstock, New York

Lee Mindel
New York, New York

Stephen Muse
Washington, D.C.

Florence Perchuk
New York, New York

Lyn Peterson
New Rochelle, New York

Travis Price III
Tacoma Park, Maryland

Ristomatti Ratia
Chicago, Illinois

Gene Reed
Nyack, New York

Michael Rex
Sausalito, California

Barbara Ross
New York, New York

Michael Rubin
New York, New York

Daen Scheiber
San Francisco, California

Sudie Schenck
Boston, Massachusetts

Barbara Schwartz
New York, New York

Peter Shelton
New York, New York

Mark Simon
Essex, Connecticut

Barbara Weinstein
New York, New York

Sue Westphal
Norwalk, Connecticut

Vicente Wolf
New York, New York

Jamie Wollens
New York, New York

Carol Zimmerman
San Antonio, Texas

*The room on page 7 was designed by William Diamond and Anthony Baratta;
page 11, Julie Atwood; page 15, Lyn Peterson and Christina Ratia; page 16,
Mark McInturff; page 30, Julie Atwood; page 42, Tricia Guild; page 52, Ted Flato;
page 74, Tricia Foley; page 100, Walter Chatham.*

PHOTOGRAPHY CREDITS

1	Elyse Lewin	70-71	Feliciano	100	Langdon Clay
7	Jeff McNamara	72	John Vaughan	102	Christopher Irion
11	John Vaughan	73	Michael Dunne (top)	104-105	Christopher Irion
15	Michael Skott		Judith Watts (bottom)	106-113	John Vaughan
16	Langdon Clay	74	Antoine Bootz	114	Walter Smalling (left)
17-18	Jeff McNamara	76-77	John Vaughan		Judith Watts (right)
20-23	Jeff McNamara	79-81	John Vaughan	115	Walter Smalling
24	William P. Steele	82-85	Jeff McNamara	116	Karen Radkai
26-29	William P. Steele	86	Kari Haavisto	117	Lizzie Himmel
30	John Vaughan	87	Antoine Bootz	118	Jeff McNamara
32-35	Kari Haaristo	88	David Montgomery	119	William P. Steele
36-37	John Vaughan	89	Scott Frances (top left)	120	Langdon Clay
39-41	John Vaughan		John Vaughan	121	Feliciano (top left)
42	David Montgomery		(bottom left)		Kari Haavisto (top right)
44	Tom Yee		Elyse Lewin (top right)		Jeff McNamara (bottom)
46-47	Tom Yee	90	Karen Radkai	122	Jeff McNamara
48-51	John Vaughan	91	Jeff McNamara	124-128	Jeff McNamara
52	Timothy Hursley	92	Feliciano	130-131	Jeff McNamara
54	Alan Weintraub	93	Michael Skott (top)	132-133	John Vaughan
56-57	Alan Weintraub		Peter Bosch (bottom)	134	Michael Dunne
58-61	Judith Watts	94	Langdon Clay	135	Jeff McNamara (left)
62-63	Robert Lautman	95	Scott Frances	136	Tim Street-Porter
64	Langdon Clay	96	Jeff McNamara	137	Elyse Lewin (top left)
65	Jacques Dirand	97	Michael Dunne (left)		Elyse Lewin (top right)
66	Antoine Bootz		Elyse Lewin (right)		Michael Skott (bottom)
67	John Vaughan	98	David Montgomery	138-139	Jeff McNamara
68	Tim Street-Porter	99	Jeff McNamara (top)		
69	Judith Watts		Joshua Greene (bottom)		

House Beautiful would like to thank the following homeowners:
Tav and Peter Berry (pages 18-23), Mike and Gina Cerre
(pages 36-41), Kiki Boucher and Aaron Shipper (pages 54-57,
114), Gigi Khoo and David Fischer (pages 58-61),
Patricia and John Carleton (page 63), Mike and Donna Bell
(page 67), Katie and Robert Langford (page 69), Tricia Foley
(pages 74, 144), Marlene Levinson (pages 76-81), Mary Gilroy
(pages 82-85), Nancy and John Calhoun (pages 86, 87),
Peter De Caprio and Noel Pasqua (page 89), Nini Reeves
(pages 90, 116), Sarina and John Mascheroni (page 92),
Mary Emmerling (page 93), Nat Hirsch (page 94), Stuart and
Judy Hagmann (page 97), Mary Florence and William Forsythe
(pages 100, 120), Sue and Richard Wollack (pages 102-105),
William Howard Adams (page 115), Barbara and Didier Wirth
(page 134), Claudia Swimmer (page 136).